MAGNIFICE

This play was first staged at the Royal Court Theatre in June 1973.
Described by the author as a 'kind of tragedy', it shows the violent collision
of two worlds – that of a group of radical protesters and a Cabinet Minister.
What began as a squatting demonstration leads to an assassination plot.
Magnificence is far from being a comfortable play but it is the work of a
playwright who seems to come closer than most to a true understanding of
the social malady of violence in Britain *now*.

'. . . it raises the kind of questions rarely debated on the modern English
stage. At what point, if ever, does violence become a legitimate political
tactic? To what extent is radical protest, without the support of the
people, a form of self-indulgence? How, if at all, does one puncture the
discreet charm of the English bourgeoisie?'

Michael Billington in *The Guardian*

'. . . it is scene for scene a wonderful piece of theatre; annexing whole new
chunks of modern life and presenting them in a style at once truthful and
magnified.'

Irving Wardle in *The Times*

*The photo on the front cover is by John Haynes and shows Kenneth
Cranham as* Jed *and Leonard Fenton as* Slaughter, *in the 1973 Royal Court
production.*

*The photograph on the back cover is reproduced by courtesy of Snoo
Wilson.*

Howard Brenton

MAGNIFICENCE

EYRE METHUEN · LONDON

First published in Great Britain 1973
by Eyre Methuen Ltd
11 New Fetter Lane, London EC4P 4EE
This edition 1980 by Eyre Methuen Ltd

Set by Expression Typesetters
Printed in Great Britain by
Whitstable Litho Limited, Whitstable, Kent

ISBN 0 413 46750 3

CAUTION
All rights whatsoever in this play are strictly reserved and application for
performance etc. should be made before rehearsal to Margaret Ramsay Ltd,
14a Goodwin's Court, St. Martin's Lane, London WC2N 4LL. No performance
may be given unless a licence has been obtained.

To Max

Sink into the mire
Embrace the butcher
But change the world.

Brecht: *Die Massnahme*

MAGNIFICENCE was first performed at the Royal Court Theatre on 28 June 1973 with the following cast:

WILL	Michael Kitchen
JED	Kenneth Cranham
MARY	Carole Hayman
VERONICA	Dinah Stabb
CLIFF	Peter Postlethwaite
CONSTABLE	James Aubrey
SLAUGHTER	Leonard Fenton
ALICE	Geoffrey Chater
BABS	Robert Eddison
OLD MAN/LENIN	Nikolaj Ryjtkov

Directed by Max Stafford-Clark
Designed by William Dudley
Lighting by Andy Phillips

Scene One

A dirty room empty but for a mound of old newspapers in the corner. Silence. Then a bang on the door. Voices off.

WILL: Bust in. Just like that.

MARY: What a smell.

JED: Let's get the stuff.

MARY: That on the stair, that a dead . . . Something?

   (A pause.)

JED: Just a bit o' rag, love.

CLIFF: Let's get the gear in.

WILL: I want a peep upstairs.

CLIFF: Give me a hand, girls.

VERONICA: Right.

   (WILL's footsteps coming up the stairs.)

JED: Dump the stuff in the hall.

   (The door tried. It won't open. The door tried more violently.)

WILL: Jed?

JED: What?

WILL: Door's stuck.

   (The door banged. JED's footsteps coming up the stairs.)

JED: Can't be.

WILL: Is.

   (The door banged.)

JED: But we looked the place over twenty-four hours ago.

WILL: The door is stuck.

   (The door banged, hard.)

JED: Don't do that!

WILL: Gotta bash it down, Jed.

JED: Can't you fiddle it? Like the front door?

WILL: Dead lock, in't it. Such locks are simple. Many an old key will flip 'em. Got an old key on you?

JED: No.

WILL: No. So.

(The door banged.)

JED: Don't do that!

CLIFF: What's up?

JED: Door's stuck.

CLIFF: But we looked the place over twenty-four hours ago.

WILL: Don't think the landlord's been round? Barred it up inside?

JED: Why should he?

WILL: Could have got wind. Of us.

JED: What barred a door, first floor, on the inside?

(The door banged.)

WILL: } That's barred.

JED: } Don't do that.

WILL: Barred. Vast iron impediments. Bet the landlord's in there, crouched in the middle o' the room with a shot gun.

VERONICA: What's up?

CLIFF: Door's stuck.

VERONICA: Wonderful.

(The door banged.)

JED: No unnecessary damage.

WILL: Theft Act 1968. Breaking and entering no offence if no larceny intended. Therefore . . .

(The door banged. A pause.)

Oh, look the doorknob's fallen off.

JED: I love you, you silly little man but I wish you wouldn't piss about . . . Don't poke it through!

(The doorknob falls onto the stage. A pause.)

You poked it through.

WILL: Well. That's the revolution. No doorknob to get in and start it.

JED: We'll go up through the window.

MARY: What you doin'?

JED: We're going up through the window.

VERONICA: What about the gear?

JED: Up through the window.

WILL: There won't be a ladder. Too much to ask of the world for there to be a ladder.

(Footsteps going down the stairs. Silence. Then their voices off, from the back.)

Well, what d'you know, a ladder. Bet its rungs are rotten!

(The end of a ladder appears, waving around outside the window. It crashes through the window. Real glass. A pause.)

I broke the window pane.

CLIFF: Malicious damage, Jed.

JED: I know. I know.

(A pause. Then WILL's head appears outside the window.)

MARY: How's it look?

WILL: Like a dirty room. Yeh a dirty room. But to me, the promised land. All manner o' birds and beasts at play in the revolutionary pastures.

JED: Hurry up, Will. There's two old ladies over the street, staring at us.

WILL: Hand the old dears a few pamphlets.

JED: Christ, Will, what's the matter?

WILL: Glass!

(He works.)

'Ang on.

(He clears the frame and climbs in. The others follow. VERONICA, MARY who's pregnant, CLIFF and JED. As long as this takes, in silence. They're in. JED puts his arm round MARY. VERONICA stands close to CLIFF. They stand there, embarrassed.)

JED: Well.

(A pause.)

Here we are.

MARY: Yeh.

WILL: Yeh. Yes.

(MARY and WILL giggle. A pause.)

VERONICA: And what happens now?

WILL: We occupy the place.

(A pause.)

CLIFF: Funny feeling.

(WILL takes out a paint spray. He writes *ANARCHY FARM* on the wall.)

WILL: That about sums it up.

MARY: Let's put our names on.

(WILL hands MARY the paint spray. They write their Christian names on the wall, all except VERONICA.)

VERONICA: What about the old ladies?

WILL: Didn't you give 'em the pamphlets?

   (During VERONICA's speech, CLIFF looks at the door.)

JED: Where's the list, love?

MARY: In the bag.

   (JED takes a clipboard out of one of the bags. He goes down the list
   carefully.)

VERONICA: The first old lady took the second old lady's pamphlet. The first
old lady then tore up her pamphlet and the second old lady's pamphlet, and
threw the pieces to the pavement. The second old lady then looked dis-
tressed, tut tutted, and bent with difficulty to pick up the pieces of paper.
All the pieces picked up, she walked briskly down the street to put them in
a litter bin by a postbox. The first old lady followed, talking. And they'll be
back.

   (WILL offers VERONICA the paint spray. She half turns away.)

WILL: Come on. A celebratory gesture?

   (VERONICA shrugs, takes the paint spray and writes her name. MARY has
   taken a flash-light polaroid from her bag. WILL strikes a pose. She takes a
   flash picture of the wall, and WILL and VERONICA before it.)

   Base camp. The journey to the Pole begins.

   (CLIFF has given up the door. It's still closed. He looks out the window.)

CLIFF: Our ladies are back.

JED: Barricade the front door, eh Cliff?

CLIFF: Right.

   (CLIFF climbs out the window. WILL goes through the lavatory door.)

JED: I'll move the stuff into the front garden. Will?

   (WILL, off.)

WILL: In the john.

JED: I'll hand the stuff into you.

WILL: 'Wonderful'.

   (The sound of CLIFF barricading the front door, heard off. VERONICA takes
   out a cigarette and lights it. MARY takes a rolled-up banner out of her bag.)

MARY: Take 'old, V.

VERONICA: What's that?

MARY: Banner.

VERONICA: Didn't know anything about a banner.

MARY: Take 'old, then.

(They begin to unfurl the banner, face down on the floor. Don't let the audience see the slogan yet.)

VERONICA: You make this thing, Mary?

MARY: Yeh.

VERONICA: What are we going to do with it?

MARY: 'Ang it out the window.

VERONICA: 'For all the World to see'?

MARY: That's the idea.

VERONICA: Why?

MARY: Why?

(Uncertain.)

To let 'em all know we're 'ere.

VERONICA: Fond of banners are you?

(A gesture at the walls.)

Graffiti?

MARY: We did a project at Art College on loo scribblers.

VERONICA: On what?

MARY: In public lavatories.

VERONICA: Good God.

MARY: Euston Station Ladies was the best.

VERONICA: I know the visual arts are in deep trouble, but that's ridiculous.

MARY: Not really. You find all kind a' agonies, scrawled out on walls.

(The banner is now unfurled.)

Oh, dear it's crinkly. Should 'ave ironed it 'fore we left.

(She moves along, tugging it top to bottom.)

Help then, V.

(VERONICA shrugs, kneels and helps to stretch the banner. CLIFF can be still heard off, nailing up the front door. VERONICA and MARY finish stretching the banner, then go to either end and lift it. The audience see the slogan for the first time. It reads: *WE ARE THE WRITING ON YOUR WALL*. WILL comes out of the lavatory.)

WILL: A very uplifting message.

VERONICA: Bit childish.

WILL: Why?

VERONICA: For one thing, it's not *on* a wall.

WILL: A bourgeois quibble, ducks.

VERONICA: How are you going to hang it up?

MARY: Outside.

(She shrugs.)

Out the window.

VERONICA: But it's huge. It'll sag.

(VERONICA droops the banner.)

WILL: It won't. It'll . . .

(A vague gesture.)

Blow about.

VERONICA: No one will read it. Just a rag, hanging there in the street. It's utterly pathetic.

(JED appears at the window, one arm round a cardboard box.)

WILL: Doing our 'umble best, Ma'am, to wreck Society.

JED: Would the wrecker of Society take hold of a box of baked beans?

(WILL goes at once to the window and takes the box. Throughout the following passage JED is continually appearing at the window with supplies and handing them to WILL. They spread out over the floor.)

MARY: V, tight again.

(They hold the banner tight.)

Yeh, the W's wonky.

(She thinks. A pause.)

Down, please.

(VERONICA and MARY lower the banner onto the floor. MARY kneels, takes out sewing things from her bag and sews the 'W'. VERONICA lights a cigarette, annoyed. A pause.)

Made the letters out o' old material my Mum 'ad. Blackout, she said. But my Mum says any bit o' old material in the 'ouse was blackout.

'That was blackout,' she says, and nods. As if saying . . . 'That'll teach you.'

I hope the black won't run. Do you think it'll run?

VERONICA: Probably. Almost certainly.

(She turns away.)

One more botched good intention, drooping in the rain.

MARY: A searchlight would be great.

VERONICA: A what?

MARY: Searchlight.

WILL: With slides?

MARY: Yeh, messages. On the 'ouses. We'd shine 'em out the window, at night.

WILL: Great.

VERONICA: Are you serious?

MARY: And on the clouds. They used to do that in the thirties. Flash up an advert at night. Suddenly all over the sky . . . Wright's Coal Tar Soap, or something.

VERONICA: What messages?

MARY: You what?

VERONICA: What messages shall we . . . Flash upon the night sky?

WILL: Something simple.

(Grandly.)

'Seize The Weapons Of Happiness.'

(Change.)

'Ere that's not bad. Where's the aerosol?

(WILL takes the paint spray from VERONICA and writes *WEAPONS OF HAPPINESS* on the wall.)

VERONICA: Alright. Alright. What are they?

(A pause. WILL writing.)

'The Weapons Of Happiness.' What are they?

WILL: 'Alf a brick through a window?

VERONICA: Is that all we have to offer?

WILL: If that is all there is to 'and, yeh . . . Bit of blackout . . . Tin of baked beans . . . Just what's to hand, and simple.

VERONICA: There is nothing simple in this brutal world, only the simple-minded.

(WILL to MARY.)

WILL: She mean me?

MARY: Yeh.

(WILL and MARY laugh.)

VERONICA: Will, I know I've come late to the group. And I wasn't with you when you argued out what to do. But don't let's write messages and slogans. If we've got to scrawl over everything, let's at least scrawl how it is. Like . . .

(She thinks.)

Like . . . After all the official figures, sums, percentages and lies there are . . .

(Writing *1,000,000* on the wall.)

MARY and WILL: Ohh . . . Ohh . . . Ohh . . .

VERONICA: Homeless in the city. And where are they? Why aren't there tents all over Hyde Park? Human foxholes in Kensington Gardens?

But the people are there, poked in somewhere. Like trying to hide litter, ramming it into the cracks in the walls. Ramming people, into cracks in the walls.

WILL: I know that. We know that. That is what we are here for. So what's the big bone of contention, lady?

VERONICA: That we've got to be clear. Not simple-minded. Clear about how it is.

WILL: Doing the best we can. Saying . . . Look at this place. Empty. And how many other places, good houses, all over the city . . . Empty.

VERONICA: But we've got to be . . .

(A short pause.)

I don't know.

Real! Real to the old ladies outside. So we can say . . . Look, it's real. The decay. The vicious city. The brutal squandering. It's real, here . . .

(She stamps.)

Down your street. Dear God it matters.

WILL: I know it matters.

VERONICA: Then don't festoon it with half-baked idiocies.

(She jerks the banner with her foot, viciously.)

MARY: Careful! You lost my needle.

WILL: Now you gone and lost this little girl's needle.

(JED at the window. The banging off, stops.)

JED: What's going on?

MARY: I lost my needle.

VERONICA: Jed. They'll look at this, ordinary people will look at this and say 'How stupid'.

WILL: It makes me feel good.

JED: It makes him feel good.

VERONICA: It'll make them feel sick.

WILL: If they're gonna spew, they're gonna spew.

VERONICA: I don't think we should put it up. We've got to be . . . Responsible.

WILL: They're gonna spew.

(MARY finds the needle.)

MARY: *There* it is.

VERONICA: Jed?

(A pause. He shrugs.)

JED: Put it up?

(He goes back down the ladder, out of sight.)

VERONICA: You want ordinary people to look at us in here and put it all down to a dose of clap and the Welfare State?

(CLIFF climbs in through the window. He is carrying pieces of wood, a bag of nails and a hammer.)

WILL: I don't mind being called a clapped-out milksop. There are worse things in this big, beautiful world to be called.

CLIFF: I've nailed up the front door.

(He kneels before the door, carefully measuring the bit of wood. JED appears at the window.)

JED: Mary, love, make some tea. The Calor gaz-stove is in the black box.

MARY: I know I packed it.

JED: Don't forget to measure out the water in cups.

MARY: I won't.

(She's cross.)

JED: You alright?

MARY: Yeh.

(JED stares at her then goes down the ladder again. A pause. VERONICA lights another cigarette. MARY sewing the 'W'. CLIFF sizing up the door. WILL takes two loads from JED, and begins to move them around. By now there are boxes and equipment out over the floor. MARY finishes sewing.)

Done.

(A pause. MARY gets the stove working, puts on a kettle.)

WILL: Can tell you work for the BBC, 'cos of the way you go on about ordinary people.

CLIFF: Give over, Will.

WILL: No I'm genuinely interested. We're going to see a lot of each other's knickers in the next few days.

(He smiles at VERONICA.)

CLIFF: Just let's have a little . . .

(A gesture, calming down.)

WILL: Why not?

(WILL imitates the gesture. A pause. Then WILL pipes up nonetheless.)

You TV skulls! Like a plague of locusts upon every hopeless good cause in sight. You only got to begin a hopeless good cause, and there you are, a dark cloud upon the horizon and soon on the poor hopeless do-gooder. Chomp chomp. Adventure playgrounds, free contraceptive clinics, school-room abortion service, chomp chomp. Hells Angels last week, geriatric wards next. And in between, why, the English Revolution, ta-rum-ta-ta. I've had you lot, I've had you sick. Marxist are you? Are you? Eh? Eh? Lot o' Marxists in the BBC I'm told. Turning out fascist crap. Argue it's the dialectic let's 'em. That dialectically straight up, it is a very good thing, straight up year in year out to turn out fascist crap. I don't think, on the whole, they are very sincere people. You can tell, the way they go on about pollution. Running through the electric corridors, pulling their hair out with worry 'bout pollution. I am probably the only man in England who is in favour of pollution. I think it's a very good idea indeed. All that lovely filth.

(He grins.)

Am I riling you? What's the thing you worked on last?

VERONICA: I worked on a documentary, about lead content, in the blood of Lancashire children.

WILL: Having heavy babies up there, are they?

(CLIFF begins to batten up the door.)

VERONICA: For Godsake.

WILL: I am riling you.

VERONICA: No, but I think I'm going to kill you. You know your trouble?

WILL: No.

VERONICA: Never mind.

WILL: Come on.

VERONICA: No.

WILL: Don't be shy. I've been abused by all kinds of people in my time. Policemen. Little children. Trotskyists. All have heaped abuse on me.

VERONICA: No.

WILL: I am so frightened of hard ladies.

VERONICA: I'm frightened of soft men.

WILL: How much do you make a year?

VERONICA: Piss off.

(She looks at CLIFF.)

WILL: That much eh? Had an argument with Cliff 'bout you coming along. Media bitch I said. Mess us up. Get us all on the box, dirty squatters, 'ow we ate off the floorboards. Had group sex 'anging from the light fixtures.

(JED appears at the window, not carrying anything. He climbs in.)

Eh, Jed, we checked there's no electric?

JED: Switch a light on and see.

WILL: No bulb.

CLIFF: Bound to be off, in't it?

(CLIFF finishes battening the door. WILL, to VERONICA.)

WILL: Got time off have you? You come an-occupyin' with us?

VERONICA: Two weeks holiday.

WILL: What if we're stuck in here longer than that?

(JED stops listening to WILL and VERONICA, and begins to sort out the supplies. A pause.)

VERONICA: I'll resign.

WILL: Ah.

VERONICA: What does that mean?

WILL: Just 'ah'.

CLIFF: Two doors they'll bash in.

WILL: Great. If you're goin' to be done by due process, may as well get well and truly done.

(VERONICA stares at CLIFF. He smiles.)

Funny. Plonkin' yourself down in London Town. Wanting all the big boots to come running.

(WILL suddenly goes down on all fours, lays an ear to the ground.)

On there, please, Mr Bailiff. Make the blood flow please, Mr Bigboot.

(WILL comes out of that. And starts to help JED.)

VERONICA: Can't we make the door harder to 'Bash in'?

CLIFF: They'll have trouble with that.

WILL: Yeh, splinter nicely.

VERONICA: But thicker wood. And screws. We could stop them.

CLIFF: Why . . . ?

WILL: . . . Why?

CLIFF: Why should we?

(A pause. VERONICA about to say something fierce, but she shrugs.)

VERONICA: For the hell of it?

WILL: Ah now that's more like it. Pricks and kicks I can understand.

(From here CLIFF and VERONICA join WILL and JED in sorting the supplies out. An effect: the supplies have come through the window, and are all about the floor. JED begins to sort them out. WILL joins them. Then suddenly they are all sorting the things out. The room becomes transformed into an orderly, indoor camp. Space out the following exchanges while this is being done.)

JED: V, tin of baked beans.

(He throws the tin to VERONICA who catches it.)

WILL: With little Frankfurters I hope. They are my favourite.

(A pause.)

VERONICA: One packet of crisps.

WILL: With or without added protein?

VERONICA: With.

(In the following passage JED is taking baked bean tins from a box tossing them to CLIFF who tosses them to MARY. Suddenly tins are flying through the air and they're all laughing.)

Condensed milk.

JED: Baked beans.

VERONICA: Corned beef.

JED: Baked beans.

VERONICA: Irish stew.

ALL: Baked beans.

VERONICA: Sardines.

ALL: Baked beans.

VERONICA: Tuna fish.

ALL: Baked beans.

VERONICA: Garden peas.

ALL: Baked beans.

VERONICA: Mixed veg.

ALL: Baked beans.

VERONICA: Spaghetti rings.

ALL: Baked beans.

VERONICA: New potatoes.

ALL: Baked beans.

VERONICA: Why so many baked beans?

WILL: Me. I love 'em.

(Handfuls of tins . . .)

MARY: What I thought was, food should be cold. Or just heated on the stove without water. Keep water for fresh drinking, you see.

VERONICA: Soup.

(She looks at a label.)

Asparagus.

(A pause. MARY with a big polythene bag. It chinks.)

MARY: Knives and forks in here.

WILL: The booze in here.

(Five cartons, with bottles in. WILL quickly taking all the bottles out, arranging them in a square on the floor.)

MARY: Don't do that, Will.

WILL: What?

MARY: Keep the bottles in the boxes.

WILL: But it's nice to see what we've got. Spread out. 'Fore we cross the Gobi Desert.

(MARY shrugs. A pause.)

VERONICA: Marmite. Strawberry jam. Apricot jam. What's this?

MARY: Rags. My Mum's got a thing about rags. If you've got to lock yourself up for weeks on end she said, you've got to have lots of rags.

VERONICA: Wise lady.

MARY: She's a silly cow.

CLIFF: Only got the three lilos. We thought the girls'll have two, and we'll argue it out.

WILL: Fair enough.

MARY: 'Ere, Will, Jed, it's like when we were in France, with the tent.

WILL: The Gypsy Life. Stars, cold water, taken short in the Camargue.

MARY: Better clear up now.

(But she doesn't move, looking at the supplies now arranged. They all look except for CLIFF, who keeps pumping a lilo. CLIFF pumps a few more times, then stops, realizing they're all looking at the supplies. A long pause.)

Got to live off that for the next . . .

(She shrugs.)

Don't look much, does it.

(A pause. Then MARY, simply.)

Like when I was a kid. We hid in a tree house. You know, few old planks, nailed up together, up in a tree. On the Common. Got smashed up, o' course. Doll's house. And tough kids came running from all over, to smash it up. But we hid up there for a while. And dogs came up, at the foot o' the tree, an' barked at us. We planned to live up there forever.

Who's gonna chuck the ladder away?

(They look at each other. Suddenly festive.)

CLIFF: Christ!

JED: Forgot that.

(He puts his arm round MARY.)

WILL: Who's going to do the honours?

(They look at JED.)

JED: V?

> (VERONICA shrugs, and goes and throws the ladder down.)

VERONICA: Isolation.

> (A rumbling sound. An OLD MAN rises from the pile of papers in the corner. He is dressed in the heavy, dirty clothes of a street dweller. He limps to the door, disregarding them. He takes out a key but is at a loss to find the door nailed up. He gestures hopelessly. Hangs his head and thinks. Rubs his hands on his coat. Then he turns and shambles across the stage, going through the door to the lavatory. All looking after him. A short silence. The light down fast.)

Scene Two

The street outside the house is painted on a drop cloth. The chanting is heard from behind the cloth. A young CONSTABLE and MR SLAUGHTER, a heavy man in his late forties, step onto the stage. They look up. For all his aggression MR SLAUGHTER shows a nervousness chewing little mints.

JED: At the sign of the Third World War.

ALL: At the sign of the Third World War, the whole structure of imperialism will collapse.

MARY: The future is bright.

ALL: The world is progressing, the future is bright.

MARY: In the end.

ALL: In the end, it is the people who are really powerful.

JED: The people.

ALL: And the people alone.

MARY: A force so swift and violent.

ALL: The people, a force so swift and violent. Will smash all the trammels that bind them.

JED: The reactionaries.

ALL: Warlords, corrupt officials, local tyrants, evil gentry.
They are blind and all is dark before them.

CONSTABLE: They're still up there, Mr Slaughter. Hymn singing.

SLAUGHTER: That what you call it?

CONSTABLE: Like a churchload of old women, singing 'All Things Bright and Beautiful'. May scare you rotten, but it don't mean anything.

SLAUGHTER: I don't see what's so scary in a church congregation.

CONSTABLE: All fanaticism, in't it.

SLAUGHTER: Is it indeed.

CONSTABLE: The beast in man.

SLAUGHTER: I beg your pardon?

CONSTABLE: The beast.

SLAUGHTER: Ah yes.

(A pause.)

CONSTABLE: You see, man's intelligence has grown so . . . Very big that he can no longer contain his animal nature. Which he retains. And that accounts for wars, criminal acts, and all other irrational behaviour.

Though there is another theory.

SLAUGHTER: Oh dear.

(A pause.)

Sleepy-bys.

(Beats his gloved hands together, blows in them.)

CONSTABLE: They on the mains up there? Got power for heating?

SLAUGHTER: Nope.

CONSTABLE: Must be very cold for them.

SLAUGHTER: I hope so. Water's cut off too. The loo must be stinking something terrible by now.

I hope.

(The CONSTABLE, embarrassed.)

CONSTABLE: Yes?

(A pause.)

Yes, we're all Martians.

SLAUGHTER: ?

(A pause.)

I'm sorry I thought you said we are all Martians.

CONSTABLE: That's the theory.

SLAUGHTER: Ah.

(A pause.)

CONSTABLE: A Russian scientist believes in it.

SLAUGHTER: Oh.

CONSTABLE: Millions of years ago, Martians landed on earth. And found apes. They doctored the apes, and made 'em think.

SLAUGHTER: Why?

CONSTABLE: What?

SLAUGHTER: Why?

CONSTABLE: Well . . . As an experiment.

SLAUGHTER: Pretty cruel.

CONSTABLE: Martians have got a higher sense of morality than us.

SLAUGHTER: They must have.

CONSTABLE: Stuck bits of their own minds in the poor apes' heads. And those apes, they're us.

(A pause. SLAUGHTER frowns.)

From time to time. Martians come down to see how we're getting on. Like Jesus.

SLAUGHTER: Jesus was . . . One of 'em, then?

CONSTABLE: Stands to reason. How else, did he ascend into Heaven?

SLAUGHTER: You tell me.

CONSTABLE: Anti-gravity drive.

SLAUGHTER: That would explain it.

CONSTABLE: They have to come down every so often, 'cos the experiment's gone wrong you see. We've run amock. Laboratory animals run amock, that's us.

SLAUGHTER: What a load of cock.

CONSTABLE: Yeh. A Russian scientist believes in it though.

SLAUGHTER: The Force has become highly philosophical since my day.

CONSTABLE: It's our Chief Constable. He's got a degree from Cambridge.

SLAUGHTER: When I was a copper, they were all leftovers from the British Raj. Wonderful men.

CONSTABLE: He's keen on us getting O Levels. I got Art. Failed English Language, though.

SLAUGHTER: Thought of leaving?

CONSTABLE: The Force?

SLAUGHTER: Made a packet since I did.

CONSTABLE: Did think of being a Security Guard. But I didn't like the uniform.

SLAUGHTER: How about my line?

CONSTABLE: I don't think I'd like being a freelance Bailiff.

SLAUGHTER: Why not? It's a healthy life. Booked a room in the Athens Hilton for our holidays this year.

CONSTABLE: That is healthy. I suppose.

SLAUGHTER: Better than piles from riding wet bicycles. That'll be your lot, my son.

CONSTABLE: We got motorbikes now. Scotts. Lovely little jobs. Watercooled, horizontally opposed cylinders, four stroke, shaft driven . . .

SLAUGHTER: Presumably rain still falls upon the saddle leather?

CONSTABLE: Trouble is, no offence, Mr Slaughter . . .

SLAUGHTER: None will be taken.

CONSTABLE: What you do, is barely legal.

(A pause.)

Mr Slaughter?

(A pause.)

You alright?

SLAUGHTER: Sorry, lad. It's just that I'm getting paranoid these days.

CONSTABLE: Ah.

SLAUGHTER: What do you mean by 'ah'? What do you mean by 'ah'?

CONSTABLE: Nothing, Mr Slaughter.

SLAUGHTER: 'Scuse me just one minute. Let me swallow three times.

CONSTABLE: Sure. G . . . Go ahead.

(A pause.)

SLAUGHTER: That's better. I've not been the same since that telly crew came round.

CONSTABLE: World In Action.

SLAUGHTER: You saw 'em crucify me, did you?

CONSTABLE: I thought it was a very fair programme.

SLAUGHTER: *Fair*?

CONSTABLE: Camera work was a bit arty.

SLAUGHTER: One.

(A pause.)

Two.

(A pause.)

Three.

(A pause.)

Learnt that trick in Kenya. Keep down your fear o' Mau Mau.

CONSTABLE: Got a bit lost with the statistics.

SLAUGHTER: It was all a grotesque distortion. For a start, I'd been up all night and hadn't shaved. No wonder I looked a villain. Also, it was totally untrue.

CONSTABLE: What, all of it?

SLAUGHTER: Every close up, hazy zoom in lens whatnot.

CONSTABLE: You never put shit through that old lady's letter box, then?

SLAUGHTER: Never.

CONSTABLE: Abduct her pussycat? Present her with an invalid eviction notice?

SLAUGHTER: You been reading the Sunday Times, haven't you?

CONSTABLE: The Chief Constable likes us to keep abreast intellectually.

SLAUGHTER: That old lady. See, she had five hundred quid from the landlord to move. It was a straightforward deal. She was the only one left in the property. Well, he wanted her out, to redevelop. All was above-board. He paid her to move, found her another place. True she lived in Chalk Farm and the new place was a ropey basement in Brixton . . . But she agreed. Come the day vacancy was due to fall. Fall upon, if you get my meaning. . .

CONSTABLE: Quite. Judgment Day.

SLAUGHTER: Yeh, time to chuck the old bag out. And what she do? Protest innocence. Deny the payment was made. Telephone Sunday papers and television news desks. I would not have thought a seventy-five-year-old spinster had it in her.

CONSTABLE: Pity she died.

(A pause.)

SLAUGHTER: One.

(A pause.)

Two.

(A pause.)

Three.

I dunno.

O.K. O.K. I was leaning upon a poor old girl, oh yes, and my mother's hair too is shining white.

But I dunno. That affray with the old lady and the pussycat cost me dear. Thirty families I had leaned on before her. At two thousand pounds a go.

CONSTABLE: Two thousand?

SLAUGHTER: Plus perks.

CONSTABLE: Dear me.

SLAUGHTER: What's the matter?

CONSTABLE: Nothing.

SLAUGHTER: I know you think I am corrupt.

CONSTABLE: No I don't . . .

SLAUGHTER: Developers buy some clapped-out two-storey pile. Ten thousand, two years back. Chuck out whoever may be living on the rat-infested floors. And today, auction in a flash West End Hotel . . .

CONSTABLE: A lot o' money?

SLAUGHTER: Thirty thousand. Maybe in a year's time, forty thousand. Well, they can spread a few quid my way.

CONSTABLE: I feel . . .

SLAUGHTER: Heady at the raz-ma-taz of it? The money pouring down the bomb-damaged walls? The gold-plated slates gleaming on the leaky roofs?

CONSTABLE: Something like that.

SLAUGHTER: Still I did make a boo-boo with the old lady and the pussy what's it. I can't say 'pussycat' again or I'll have to swallow.

CONSTABLE: What exactly . . . Did go wrong there?

SLAUGHTER: Sentiment. Female, white-haired white-skinned and a lover of . . . Furry animals.

(He swallows.)

CONSTABLE: What were the other thirty families you evicted?

SLAUGHTER: Pakis, that kind of thing.

(The CONSTABLE sniffs.)

You sniff at me?

CONSTABLE: No, no, Mr Slaughter.

(A pause. They're looking up.)

SLAUGHTER: I dunno.

(A pause.)

I just do not know.

(A pause.)

I'm getting old. Can't see the world in black and white no more.

(A pause.)

According to my old Dad, the great enemy was Bertrand Russell. He'd rage on for hours, 'bout how Bertrand Russell was putting round ideas of free love on the order of Moscow.

When was that. Before the War? First or Second? The world was simple then. Clear who you had to hate and bash. Bertrand Russell and the commies.

(A pause.)

My Dad was a copper. Visions open before me, that my life has been ruined by that old man, my father. Still got a photo at home, of me on my fifth birthday. Dressed up in his helmet down to my chin, truncheon in my puny hand.

(Shades his eyes with one hand, mimes holding a truncheon in the other.)

Don't shuffle, Constable.

CONSTABLE: Sorry, Sir. I mean, Mr Slaughter.

SLAUGHTER: Am I becoming maudlin?

CONSTABLE: Oh . . . No, not really.

SLAUGHTER: Sorry, Lad. Don't blame you. Who wants to love an ageing Bailiff on the slide?

CONSTABLE: See it from my point of view, Mr Slaughter. We are both the law, and must act in concert. But you are a private sector, I am a public sector. Er . . .

(Looks about. Touches his nose, meaning 'savvy'.)

SLAUGHTER: Oh, I am embarrassing you.

CONSTABLE: I'm very . . . Flattered to talk to you.

SLAUGHTER: You're nervous I'm going to make another boo-boo.

CONSTABLE: No, Mr Slaughter, please I don't want to offend.

SLAUGHTER: No offence.

CONSTABLE: I just don't want you to get out of hand. *Things* to get out of hand.

SLAUGHTER: Ah.

CONSTABLE: Have you been drinking?

(A pause.)

SLAUGHTER: Does it show?

CONSTABLE: Smell it from here. Sir.

SLAUGHTER: I've been sucking mints for the last half hour.

(SLAUGHTER, a violent change.)

Buffooon. Sucking mints. I am a heavy man, why should I lick arses? They even have a laugh at me down at Shelter. 'Billy Boy's going in again,' they cry. And laugh. A bogey for do-gooders, that's me.

Well.

(A pause.)

Well.

(A pause.)

I tell you.

(The CONSTABLE, scared.)

CONSTABLE: What?

SLAUGHTER: I tell you, there is not a man alive, I'd vote for.

CONSTABLE: No?

SLAUGHTER: Not a man alive. Fit to have my ballot slip.

CONSTABLE: Oh.

SLAUGHTER: They see me coming. A comedy routine. 'Here comes the Bailiff big and tall, to do us all no good at all.'

Alright! Alright!

But I tell you, I've got murder in my heart.

CONSTABLE: I believe you have, Mr Slaughter.

(SLAUGHTER nods to himself.)

SLAUGHTER: Yes. That's a way of putting it. Murder.

(A pause. Suddenly he produces a court paper.)

Order issued for the eviction of that lot. Under the High Court Rule number one one three.

CONSTABLE: The old one one three, eh.

SLAUGHTER: The Bailiff's charter, mate.

(Fiercely.)

I am going to pull this off. One last stroke. Ousting our fervent friends up there. I am going to bust that lot, cleanly, utterly. A matter of wounded pride.

CONSTABLE: Like Achilles in his tent.

SLAUGHTER: What you bloody well say?

CONSTABLE: Nothing.

(A pause.)

Listen, dawn chorus.

(SLAUGHTER looks at the CONSTABLE with disgust. A pause. The CONSTABLE, nervously.)

Sending your boys in then?

SLAUGHTER: First light. 'Fore the shoppers are out. Providing the mood is right. And something tells me it's going to be.

(The CONSTABLE nervously.)

CONSTABLE: I have been detailed, Mr Slaughter. No breach of the peace.

SLAUGHTER: Don't worry. I'm a professional. A good dustman. Just pick the bin up, and *bang*.

CONSTABLE: Oh.

(Frowns.)

Good.

Scene Three

The room. It is now in chaos. On the walls rows of polaroid photographs. Dawn light growing through the window, VERONICA is awake smoking. The OLD MAN, huddled in a blanket, crouches watching her cigarette. A pause.

MARY wakes up.

MARY: Been awake long?

VERONICA: Yes.

MARY: We still got those codeine?

VERONICA: No. You alright?

MARY: Got a bit of a headache.

(A pause.)

VERONICA: We had another visitor.

MARY: What?

(VERONICA points to a turd lying on the stage.)

Oh no. Not another turd.

VERONICA: It arrived at first light.

MARY: The paper boy again?

VERONICA: I heard him laugh as he ran away.

MARY: Little bleeder, I'd love to thump him.

VERONICA: He's getting sophisticated. Can't be easy to catapult dogshit through a broken window, and this is the third time he hasn't missed.

How are you?

MARY: O.K. You?

VERONICA: It's the grot. The . . . Granular nastiness of it all. Got under my eyelids.

(She stubs her cigarette out. The OLD MAN scuttles forward, picks up the stub and scuttles back. VERONICA ignores him.)

Look at it. Liberation City.

MARY: Yeh. I dunno 'ow it gets so . . . Tumbled up. Spend most of the day cleanin'.

VERONICA: I've got so many blackheads my skin's beginning to creak.

MARY: Want me to pop 'em for you?

VERONICA: That would be kind.

MARY: Lie over then.

(She lies over in MARY's lap.)

VERONICA: In between the shoulder blades.

OLD MAN: Fuggin'? Fuggin'?

(The OLD MAN makes a gesture of striking a light.)

MARY: What's he want?

VERONICA: Ignore him.

OLD MAN: Fuggin'?

VERONICA: He just wants a light. We have this relationship. I sit there smoking through the small, mean hours. He glares from his mouldy blanket, not at my tits in the moonlight, but at the fag butts I stub on the floorboards. I'm glad we gave up trying to explain to him just what the fuck we're doing. We 'social activists' . . . We're just a passing phenomena, which leaves fag butts on the floor.

(OLD MAN, his match lighting gesture.)

OLD MAN: Fuggin'?

VERONICA: Free the land Mr! The social spaces Mr!

OLD MAN: Fuggin'?

(VERONICA throws a box of matches at the OLD MAN. He touches his forehead.)

VERONICA: Ow!

MARY: Sorry. Big one. Want a look?

(MARY shows VERONICA her thumbnail.)

VERONICA: Gosh.

MARY: Left a bit of a pit I'm afraid.

(Pause.)

You know what V?

VERONICA: What?

MARY: I like you.

VERONICA: How do you mean?

(MARY laughs.)

MARY: That make your flesh crawl?

VERONICA: Yes. Sorry.

MARY: Big one coming up now.

VERONICA: Oh God . . .

MARY: Hold your breath . . . Pop.

(A pause.)

VERONICA: Didn't feel a thing.

(A pause.)

Mary, have you thought . . . You may have it here?

MARY: What?

VERONICA: The baby. Have you thought that it may . . . Come on while we're in this place?

MARY: I'm only six months. It's not even viable yet.

VERONICA: Viable?

MARY: Doctor's word. You're not viable 'til you're seven months. And if you lose your baby after six months, they call that an abortion. And if you lose it after seven months, they call that a miscarriage.

You ever thought of 'aving a baby, V?

VERONICA: I'm on the pill.

MARY: I went on the pill, but I got fat. And fed up. So Jed and I thought.

(A pause.)

VERONICA: It's just . . . Not the right time for it.

MARY: How d'you mean?

VERONICA: It seems more . . .

(Bitterly.)

Apt.

MARY: What, to be barren?

VERONICA: 'To be barren.'

MARY: Oh V.

VERONICA: Have I shocked you?

MARY: No . . .

(A pause.)

What, you mean 'cos of ecology?

VERONICA: God no.

MARY: I dunno. The Sahara Desert's gettin' bigger every year, you know. Then there's the bomb.

(They laugh.)

VERONICA: For Godsake.

(A pause.)

No. I can't express myself.

(A pause.)

I feel a daughter at my skirts would be . . . Obscene. It would be her happiness. I couldn't stand that. I can't bear the happiness of kids. Three years old, and everything new . . . And language just come . . . Voracious little animals, gobbling the World down. *This* world. It's obscene.

MARY: Crikey, V. You do think yourself into funny corners.

VERONICA: Yes I do. Don't I.

(A pause.)

I envy you Mary. The point is . . . It's easy for you. You just arrive at things naturally. Like when we came through that window ten days ago . . . You just came through that glass . . . Blithely.

And I envy you.

(MARY annoyed.)

MARY: Ta very much.

VERONICA: What's the matter?

MARY: You . . . Twist things up.

(VERONICA turns, and holds MARY's arms.)

VERONICA: I'm sorry, Mary . . .

MARY: I don't hate you. I just . . . Hate to hear you. Not what you say, but the sound of what you say.

(She tries a little laugh.)

I hate it.

VERONICA: Yes.

(A pause.)

Yes. 'The voice of my accursed, human education.'

(JED wakes up and sits up. MARY nods at the turd.)

JED: Oh no. Will!

(A pause.)

Will! Wake up.

WILL: Help!

(WILL wakes up.)

What? What?

JED: Turd. And it's your turn.

(WILL springs out of his sleeping bag.)

WILL: The world come to us again, 'as it?

MARY: I'd better put the kettle on.

(MARY gets up and puts the kettle on the camping stove. VERONICA turns to CLIFF.)

VERONICA: Hey you.

(CLIFF turns over.)

They've formed a Committee of Public Safety and they're shooting

Members of Parliament in Trafalgar Square.

(CLIFF turns over.)

Oy Mister. Trotsky lives.

(CLIFF grunts. And suddenly wakes up.)

CLIFF: 'Morning.

VERONICA: Good morning.

(CLIFF wipes his eyes and sees the turd.)

CLIFF: Another . . .

VERONICA: Indeed.

CLIFF: His turn.

(CLIFF points at WILL and gets up. VERONICA gets up, and scratches.)

VERONICA: Sure that was the last of the Calamine two days ago?

MARY: Yeh. Sorry.

(They brush their teeth around a saucepan. MARY finishes, then VERONICA JED and CLIFF begin to shave. WILL hunts for the dustpan and brush.)

VERONICA: Baby jerks?

MARY: O.K.

VERONICA: Got the book?

(MARY tosses a book to VERONICA. It's *The New Childbirth* by Erna Wright. WILL comes forward with a dustpan and brush and a scrap of newspaper.)

Ugh, the photos in this thing.

(She reads.)

'As the baby is born she turns slightly and is quite difficult to grasp because she is slippery.'

MARY: Lesson five. Page fifty-one.

VERONICA: Fifty-one. 'Sit on the floor tailor fashion.'

(MARY does.)

They say a cushion.

(VERONICA quickly gets a blanket and folds it for MARY who sits on it.)

'The exercise you are about to learn will help to increase the suppleness of the pelvic floor.'

MARY: Yeh.

VERONICA: 'It is really an exercise taught and practised by dancers. For our purpose though, it is done in reverse.'

(MARY less certain.)

MARY: Yeh.

WILL: The turd of their malcontent.

(WILL goes to the window with the turd in the dustpan. He's about to throw it out, but stops.)

They're there.

(A pause.)

They're all there.

(At once JED, CLIFF and VERONICA go to the window and look down into the street. MARY stays sitting tailor-fashion, staring at the OLD MAN.

At last he lights the cigarette butt, and takes a drag. He stares at MARY. Suddenly he offers her a drag. MARY shakes her head, shyly.

A pause.

Then WILL throws the turd out of the window, throws the dustpan down and smacks his hands.)

Turn the bugs over? Bug hunt eh? Come on, come on, let's stir up the little bleeders . . .

(WILL turns over the bedding violently.)

If it's the last thing I'm gonna do it's see one of 'em . . . There! There! No.

(WILL stops momentarily, waves his hand before his eyes.)

Flecks on the old cornea.

(JED and CLIFF go back to shaving. MARY pulls the book toward her. WILL turns over the bedding.)

MARY: Put the soles of yer feet together . . .

(She does so. Grasps her feet together with one hand and puts the other hand under her knee. She pushes her hand towards the floor with her leg and then brings the leg to its previous position with her hand. She reads aloud, carefully.)

'The muscles on the outer side of the thigh are pulling against the muscles on the inner side, which are called the *abductors*.'

VERONICA: Stop it, stop it. Stop stop stop.

(A pause. They look at her.)

Oh God I want a bath.

(A pause.)

They're getting ready to bust their way in. Bust us. They're going to come through that door . . . And what are we doing? Nothing. What have we done? Nothing. Zero . . . Sat it out in a grubby room the grubby end of London, for what? Fag butts for him?

(The OLD MAN touches his forehead.)

OLD MAN: Fuggin'.

(VERONICA near tears.)

VERONICA: Liberation City?

(She draws back the tears.)

I loathe us. I loathe all the talks we had. That we'd really do it. Come down to the people whom it really hits . . . And do it for them. I loathe us, I loathe our stupid, puerile view of the World . . . That *we* have only to do it, that *we* have only to go puff, and the monster buildings will go splat . . . I loathe us, I loathe what we've descended to here . . . Our domesticity . . . Ten days with the fleas and the tin opener lost, never for once questioning . . . That we are in any way changing the bloody, bleeding ugly world . . . Direct action? For us it's come down to sitting on a stinking lavatory for ten days . . . Why didn't we get the local people on our side? Oh we bawled a few slogans at passers-by. Got the odd turd back from the street, and philosophized there upon. But 'Mobilize the people?' We can't mobilize a tin opener . . .

WILL: Still lost, is it?

(At WILL, fiercely.)

VERONICA: Not a tin opener, let alone real people . . . Out there.

(Quietly.)

I think we're done for. I think we're dead.

JED: What did you expect?

MARY: 'To make the muscles covering the *back* of the pelvis more subtle, push your buttocks out backwards — like a duck lifting its tail.'

VERONICA: For Godsake Mary!

MARY: I don't know about you, but I'm pregnant. So piss off.

(MARY, intent, on the book, sits back on her heels.)

JED: I dunno. Maybe we should have come down here like a carnival . . . Bonfires for the kids, landlords burning . . . I dunno.

(At once there is a fearsome crackle of a loudspeaker from outside, which doesn't work too well.

SLAUGHTER's voice through it. The group move and sit close together, during his speech.)

MICROPHONE: This . . . This is a Court Bailiff, authorized . . . What? . . . Constable, this machine . . . What? Crackles don't it, listen to it crackle . . .

(A roar, he's blowing on the mike.)

What? . . . I did blow on it . . . I'll blow on it again . . .

(A roar. Silence. And the microphone comes on again.)

Right you boys and girls in there . . . In that building . . . This is a Court Bailiff, Bailiff of the Court . . . What the bloody hell is the matter with this thing . . . Knob? What knob? . . .

(The microphone gets louder . . . more frightening.)

Right you boys and girls . . . Right! You are in unlawful occupancy of private property . . . I am authorized to eject you . . . Constable this instrument is right out of hand, ramshackle electrical equipment getting in the way of a job . . . It's going to go badly, I can feel it's going to go badly . . .

(The roar twice.)

Now I am sending my boys up to you . . . Please co-operate with them . . . Don't let's have any trouble, boys and girls, eh? You have made your point . . . Whatever it may be . . . But you have made your.

(A loud click. Silence. The group in the room have begun to smile, then laugh together. The OLD MAN huddles, hiding his face. A great blow, off . . . It's the Bailiff's men, coming through the front door.

VERONICA chants from the *Thoughts of Mao*. Leafing back and forth through the book. Each line increases their hysterical laughter.)

VERONICA: We will be ruthless to our enemies!

(A blow.)

We must have power, and annihilate them!

(A blow.)

Not to have a correct political point of view is like having no soul!

(A blow.)

The crimson path!

(A blow.)

Thousands upon thousands!

(A blow.)

Heroically laid down their lives for the people!

(A blow.)

March along the path, crimson with the blood!

(A blow.)

Do not be deluded!

(A blow.)

Do not be deluded!

(A blow.)

Do not be deluded by the outward strength of the aggressors!

(A blow. Laughter and tears. Tears.)

Go to the masses!

(A blow.)

From the masses to the masses!

(A blow.)

Go to them! Help them!

(A blow. A splintering. People blundering up the stair.)

Help them to achieve liberation and happiness!

(A blow on the door in the room. It flies open. SLAUGHTER walks in.)

SLAUGHTER: Don't let's all get carried away.

(JED points at SLAUGHTER, soundless with laughter. The CONSTABLE comes in. That's too much for JED.)

Can I share . . . The joke?

(A silence. At once the laughter leaves the actors. They wait until the theatre is silent. Then the CONSTABLE sees the Calor gaz-stove, with the soup cooking on it.)

CONSTABLE: Better have that out. Fire hazard.

(He kneels and turns the Calor gaz-stove off. From this action there springs the incident in which MARY loses her child. The CONSTABLE stands, and steps back into WILL. The CONSTABLE falters, and goes down on one knee. WILL kicks him once, and backs away with a curiously apologetic gesture. The CONSTABLE grabs WILL, and pulls him. WILL falls over MARY. SLAUGHTER kicks MARY not WILL. SLAUGHTER immediately realizes what he's done.)

SLAUGHTER: No. No. No.

(The actors freeze in a tableau. The lights change. Dark shadows from bright lights low across the tableau. An effect of a sudden negativing, and X-ray. The blows throughout JED's speech are made by the actors stamping and a drum offstage. JED speaks aside to the audience.)

JED: And they came through.

(A blow.)

Oh did they all come through.

(A blow.)

Slaughter and his boys.

(A blow.)

The Bailiff and his boys, with their great big boots.

(A blow.)

With spite and relish, beyond the call of duty.

(A blow.)

They came through.

(A blow.)

And came through us.

(A blow.)

And bust us.

(A blow.)

Oh they broke us, broke us good.

(A blow.)

Our little Wendy House.

(A blow.)

Our little Wendy House of good intent.

(A blow.)

Trod on our toys.

(A blow.)

Trampled all over our model farm.

(A blow.)

All the toy animals, killed them. Smashed their tiny delicate bones.

(A blow.)

True story.

We took over an empty house. Talked of liberating it for the poor. We were innocents.

Bailiffs broke in, beat us up. My wife was with child. They booted her, my wife's beautiful baby bulging tummy, booted. She lost the child.

(MARY cries quietly then is silent.

Light's going down. A spot on JED.)

True story from London Town. I got nine months in prison, got hooked. Hooked up, strung up, all up, *right up there*. Speed. On speed. A dangerous and proscribed drug, Sir and Madam. To the scandal and enlightenment of lost souls, freely circulating in Her Majesty's prisons. The speedy brain rotter, activator of the dark, the mighty mover, the killer action.

(A pause.)

And nine a.m., one clear day . . . Came out the little prison door in the big prison door.

Released.

Honed down.

Pure.

Angry.

(Blackout.

Interval.)

Scene Four

A bare, bright stage. Dappled sunlight to one side. ALICE there. He speaks aside.

ALICE: Early morning garden. Cambridge College. A lovely day.

(BABS comes on. He's an older man, in an academic gown. A dark suit. He walks with a stick.)

BABS: Alice!

ALICE: Babs!

(Shaking hands.)

BABS: Nice of you to come up, Alice.

ALICE: Nice of you to have me come up, Babs.

(Aside.)

Thinking, I wonder what the old man wants?

(BABS aside.)

BABS: Thinking, I piddle and he comes running.

(To ALICE.)

Shall we walk?

(They walk.)

And what news from the throbbing heart of the national groin, to torpedo my own metaphor?

ALICE: I'm sorry?

BABS: What's happening in the Cabinet these days?

ALICE: Oh, tedium. No one talking to anyone else.

BABS: And our National Saviour?

ALICE: Full of beans for the job. His words.

BABS: Mmm . . .

(A pause.)

Effortless dignity, in a flurry.

ALICE: I'm sorry?

BABS: That's what the local papers said, when I lots my constituency. 'He bowed out of public life with effortless dignity, in a flurry of optimism for new horizons.'

ALICE: Babs, why did you want to see me?

BABS: All in good time all in good time, dear. Don't get fidgety.

(Aside.)

Thinking, he's all shiny and bright! Either the aura of high office, or a sunlamp.

(ALICE, aside.)

ALICE: Thinking, he's playing the Elder Statesman out to grass disgracefully.

(BABS, aside.)

BABS: Thinking, sunlamp, because his pores are standing out. Just like him to turn up, blazing away by artificial means.

(ALICE, aside.)

ALICE: Thinking, I hope the old man's not gone gaga. There's something bad with his eye, there, it's wandering. My mother's eye wandered, when she lost her mind. Oh God, what am I going to do if he's gone gaga?

(BABS, aside.)

BABS: Thinking, and he was young and golden in the heyday of his youth. And once he deeply moved me. And now? Bloody breakfast cereal. Sunshine wrapper. Threepence off. Worthless gift inside. Still as the saying goes 'I did love her once.' And now must make some crass, appalling gesture. Last kiss, wave a hanky. In my circumstances.

(To ALICE.)

Effortless dignity.

Actually I cried. I raged and screamed. Threw a terrible scene at the third recount. No, I did not go gentle into the House of Lords.

ALICE: The seat's back with us now.

BABS: And my nephew sitting on it. Utter nincompoop. In the eighteenth century, our family was prone to syphilis. Its effects appear to have popped up again in that poor boy.

ALICE: He's doing well on Ways and Means.

BABS: The firmament gasps.

(A pause. ALICE glances at his watch.)

ALICE: How do you like it at Corpus?

BABS: Like a rick in the rectum.

ALICE: I thought the academic life appealed.

BABS: As piles in the passage.

(He points.)

That is the new College building.

ALICE: Ah.

BABS: What do you make of it?

ALICE: Sub Le-Corbusier.

BABS: What?

ALICE: Ugly.

BABS: It's got a damn good laundry.

ALICE: Ah.

BABS: What?

ALICE: Nothing, nothing.

BABS: We had a survey of college laundry.

ALICE: That's . . . Intriguing.

BABS: Turned out ninety percent of undergraduates foul their sheets. The other ten percent don't sleep in sheets at all. Thought the least I could do was argue for a laundry. Free washing machine, free bleach. My legacy to Res Academia! A plentiful supply of chemicals, to irradicate young men's semen stains.

I hate the young men of the University. No grace. All contempt. Jargon spewers, or silent vacuous eyes. One, a jargon spewer, put me through an intelligence test. Do you know my mental age?

Eight and a half.

He showed me the calculations, at my mild protest. I couldn't understand them. Having a mental age of eight and a half . . .

Rest.

ALICE: Sorry?

BABS: Rest a moment.

(BABS leans on ALICE's arm.)

ALICE: I'm sorry to find you . . . Bitter.

BABS: I am bitter.

ALICE: You know, a great many look back to what you did.

BABS: Did?

ALICE: For the country.

BABS: That came out with a thunderous clap of insincerity.

ALICE: True though. You're . . . Sorely missed.

BABS: You trying to be sarky?

ALICE: We miss your steadying influence.

BABS: Oh do shut up! My flesh is crawling. I know the depths to which I have fallen.

(BABS walks on a little. Stops.)

I'm dying.

(ALICE. Behind him.)

ALICE: I'm sorry?

BABS: Didn't you hear?

ALICE: Didn't quite catch . . . What you said.

BABS: Oh sod. Been looking forward to this moment for weeks. And I ballsed it up. Sod.

ALICE: I really didn't catch . . . Your remark.

BABS: I'm dying.

(A pause.)

ALICE: What . . .

BABS: What have I got?

ALICE: No, I mean . . .

(A pause.)

Oh God.

BABS: Absurdly gauche of me. Both the deed and the telling.

Had in the back of my mind, some great, dignified gesture.

Spend a pleasant day with you. Sunny morning on the backs. Lunch. Come evening, some gentle sunset scene. Some . . . Falling cadence.

Then I go and blurt it out in a fit of pique. Bet you didn't even realize I was piqued, just then. Well I was. And I blurted it out.

ALICE: Is . . . This definite?

BABS: I'm pregnant alright. For your peace of mind, the disease is disgusting.

ALICE: Is there anything I can do?

BABS: Spend the day with me.

ALICE: Yes.

BABS: Good.

(ALICE embarrassed, a slight cough.)

That's a nasty cough.

ALICE: Summer cold. Caught a chill at Maudy's last weekend . . .

BABS: You should wrap up well.

ALICE: Yes.

(A pause.)

BABS: Delicious!

ALICE: What?

BABS: The embarrassment. Ever since it got round the College that I was falling apart . . . Actually I put my condition round, left photocopies of my doctor's report in a few key places . . . Ever since, cavernous pauses have followed me. It's reached gigantic proportions in the Senior Common Room. Every remark, you can see the minds panicking — oh God, have I punned on his disease?

ALICE: You . . . Seem to be enjoying yourself.

BABS: On the contrary. I am full of fear, and loathing.

(Change.)

Right! River!

ALICE: What?

BABS: Punt!

ALICE: Ought you?

BABS: Don't be such an old woman. Come on!

(He goes off, spritely. For a moment ALICE hangs behind. Frowns, hand to the bridge of his nose. Then follows. A pause. They glide back onto the stage in a punt. ALICE poling. They have been drinking.)

ALICE: Don't wobble!

BABS: Not me wobbling!

ALICE: You are wobbling!

BABS: *I am not wobbling!*

ALICE: Don't, just don't!

BABS: It's a question of balance, you fool!

ALICE: I know it's a question of balance!

BABS: Let me pole!

ALICE: Don't move!

BABS: Can't stand up. Hope my inner ear's not gone. Remember in the war, shell-shocked lads, falling, and lurching, endless retching.

(Points, suddenly.)

That a corpse in the river?

ALICE: Just an old tyre.

(Manipulating the punt at the front of the stage.)

I'll pull into the bank.

(He does so. Sits in the punt. A pause.)

BABS: Alice.

(A pause.)

Are we drunk?

ALICE: Very.

BABS: That would explain it.

ALICE: What?

BABS: I suddenly had an overwhelming urge to join the Roman Catholic Church.

One moment. I'll breathe regularly and the feeling will go.

(A pause.)

That's better. Avoid that, at all cost. Taken a terrible toll amongst my contemporaries, Catholicism. Many bright young things of the right have ended up old men, wetting themselves with the joy of redemption. Ex-communist poets go that way too, so I'm told.

(He hiccups.)

Oh dear. I'm in a terrible state.

(He takes out a handkerchief.)

Look I've dribbled. Hope to God there are no Maoist Undergraduates, lurking in the bushes. They're the worst you know, the Maoist Undergraduates.

(Stretches his eyes to slits.)

Jaundiced eye-balls.

(A pause. Sly.)

Get your phone call in?

ALICE: Phone call?

BABS: Put off your meeting this afternoon.

ALICE: Ah. Yes.

BABS: Ha!

ALICE: What's funny?

BABS: I do think you're almost there.

ALICE: And 'where' would that be?

BABS: Wishing that I would . . .

(A gesture.)

Plop.

ALICE: You're disgracefully drunk.

BABS: I'm dying.

ALICE: Cheers.

BABS: They will you know. Our monstrous observers hidden upon these banks. Steaming with indignation, watching their enemies at play. They will . . .

(A gesture.)

Inherit the earth.

ALICE: Improbable.

BABS: I wonder if it's really there.

ALICE: What?

BABS: China.

ALICE: I doubt it.

BABS: It is not the perfection of the idea I fear, but its imperfection.

(A pause.)

My all-purpose quotation on Marxism-Leninism.

ALICE: Rather fatuous.

BABS: Do you think so? Do you really think so?

ALICE: Yes.

BABS: Oh dear.

ALICE: I'm sorry.

BABS: No no.

(A pause.)

Key sentence of a speech I made to the United Nations in nineteen fifty-two actually. Rather thought it was what got me the job here. Not as rotund as Winnie's 'An iron curtain has rung down . . . ' More abstract, wouldn't you say? Moral?

'Iron . . . ' 'Rung'. 'Yron, rrung.' Where did the old bag get her lovely words from?

ALICE: Natural talent?

BABS: That, perhaps. And a profound contempt for the rest of us. The rhetorican's contempt for his listeners. A warping of meaning, even elementary gist, anything for that quiver, the rattle of a million tiny bones in a million inner ears . . . Got trouble in my inner ear, by the way. Keel over sometimes . . . described the sensation to a student of mine. 'Like' he said, 'a natural high'. Get the same effect if you hold your nose, tight, and blow . .

(A pause.)

Go on.

(A pause.)

ALICE: What?

(He's not been listening.)

BABS: Have a go.

ALICE: ?

BABS: With your nose.

ALICE: Oh?

BABS: Pinch both nostrils.

(He does so. ALICE follows.)

Now blow.

(They blow.)

Hard! Really hard! Pop your ears.

(A long pause. Both blowing. ALICE lets go, BABS lets go. A pause. They both suddenly lie back. A pause. From offstage, a languid musical scale on a xylophone. An area of the stage darkens a little. Pause.)

Corrupter of youth. In the latter days of his Cabinet career, he farted a great deal. It was the first shadow of the disease which killed him. The Cabinet Room was flooded with an odour of death, adjourning many a discussion in unseemly haste. With this eccentricity, he contributed a minor but consistent influence for the bad upon the many blunders made by the Government, of which he was a distinguished member.

(A pause.)

I'm speculating upon my Obituary in the Times.

Don't seem to be getting it quite right.

(A pause.)

Corrupter of youth.

(A pause.)

Um.

(A pause.)

Outrageous old queen, happily no longer with us.

(A pause.)

Um.

(A pause.)

What do they do with Ex-Cabinet Ministers, who are queer and dead? There should be some . . . Splendid event, should there not? Some massive cere-monial. A number of masturbatory images rise up. Ten thousand working men, jeering sweetly . . . The mind wanders . . . But the Ministry of Works would foul it up. Terribly butch lot. Commit some grave error of taste. Nude Guardsmen riding bareback . . . The mind wanders, appalled.

(The xylophone scale. Another area of the stage darkens a little. A pause.)

Alice?

(He raises himself a little, looks at ALICE.)

How did you get that absurd nickname? I remember. Some bad joke about Wonderlands.

(He lies back.)

Ah Alice, fair Alice. Is that Elder Statesman hair real?

(Peers foward.)

Ha! Due for tinting the roots I see. No no, mustn't go on like that. These may be my last moments, don't want to spend them bitching. But I have, all day.

Bitched. And I invited him up, some . . . Wild notion of delivering my
political testament, and all I've done is bitch.

(He lies back, looking at ALICE. Airily, but with care . . .)

You came from the Army and Oxford. Credentials shining like an angel.
To London Clubs and your nineteen fifty-one constituency, somewhere
indeterminately the wrong side of Leicester. A dull area, which you didn't
see much. But you were bright! The old Tory Guard looked at you, all bright
and in your early thirties. You caught their glance, and greyed your eye-
brows to make you older . . . No no, mustn't bitch. Must get this right . . .
With your eyes browed grey, and your firm young neck, you were one-up
for minor ministerial rank. All the Cabinet of that time had rolling double
chins. 'Cept for myself . . .

(Pats his chin, then cross with himself . . .)

No no! Last day alive, must achieve some reasonably elevated level . . . Get
up there, somehow . . .

(Composes himself.)

And so to Junior Ministry. Angelic whizz kid of your age, you spoke
smoothly and with concern, of Tory utopias of efficiency. At garden fetes,
the silky calved wives of aldermen, told you you were so right about . . .
Fishing limits? England's role in the world? And oh, the sun rose over the
wrong side of Leicester, to touch your shoulders as you stood, atop your
campaign van in the General Election of nineteen fifty-nine. A little quiff
in the breeze of hair already artificially mature, a phrase about Britain
Going Forward, and an increase of your majority by six thousand or so.
And so . . . To inner councils. Matters of moment. In and out of famous
doors, to flashlight bulbs and puny hurrahs of tourist crowds. Ah silky,
you are silky. It's all in the throat. On television your honeyed words have a
silicone effect. Coating the tube with a silvery slime. You are a politician.

You have never had a political thought in your life.

(Raises himself. An effort here, for the first time.)

And, Alice my dear, you are a fascist. Oh, I don't mean jackboots and
Gotterdammerungs. You are a peculiarly modern, peculiarly English kind
of fascist. Without regalia. Blithe, simple-minded and vicious. I hate you.
You scare me sick. Mao had better come quick, for I think there's a danger,
a very real and terrible danger, that *you* may inherit the earth.

(A swallow, a deep breath, he kicks ALICE.)

Wake up!

ALICE: What?

BABS: You fell asleep, you thoughtless bugger.

ALICE: I feel dreadful.

BABS: Could have had the decency to stay awake.

ALICE: I'm sorry.

(Feels his head.)

Is there an Alka Seltzer?

BABS: No there is not an Alka Seltzer. I'm very upset.

ALICE: Why?

BABS: No there is not an Alka Seltzer!

ALICE: Alright, it doesn't matter.

BABS: Fascist!

ALICE: I beg your pardon?

BABS: Nothing.

ALICE: We'd better go back. Are you cold?

BABS: Yes I'm cold.

ALICE: We'll go back.

BABS: No we will not.

ALICE: We ought to.

BABS: No we will not! We'll stay up all night. Disport ourselves in the meadows. In the villages.

Come my beloved.

Let us go forth into the field;
Let us lodge in the villages.
Let us go up early to the vineyards;
Let us see whether the vine hath budded, and its blossom be open,
And the pomegranates be in flower.

The Song of Songs.

ALICE: Just stay where you are, I'll punt from this end.

BABS: I beg of you, I beg of you. No.

(Grabs ALICE's hands. ALICE sits reluctantly.)

ALICE: Alright, Babs.

(From here a long fade of the light. Imperceptible at first, to the end of the scene. A pause.)

BABS: I can't feel anything.

(A pause.)

Yes I can. There's a nail in this boat, sticking into my behind.

ALICE: Let me move you . . .

BABS: Oh no. I appear to have some . . . Equilibrium like this. Do not disturb it, or I may really, finally, fall apart.

(A pause.)

ALICE: Are you . . . Comfortable?

BABS: You mean 'In pain?'

ALICE: Yes.

BABS: 'Yes' is the answer.

ALICE: Babs we ought to go back . . .

BABS: Embarrassed?

ALICE: Let's be sensible.

BABS: Got a better idea. Tip me in the river.

ALICE: Don't be ridiculous.

BABS: Go on.

ALICE: You're being ridiculous.

BABS: Do it myself, if I had the strength.

    (ALICE holds the bridge of his nose. In a worried temper.)

ALICE: No.

BABS: Don't think I've not tried it, the last six months. A terrible series of farcical attempts. Thwarted at every turn. Pajama cords snapping in the middle of the night, that kind of thing.

    The news that I wanted to bump myself off, got round the undergraduate body. Boat club night, the darling boys hanged me in effigy outside the lodge. Sweet of them.

    Am I living every moment of this?

    (ALICE, bitterly.)

ALICE: To the hilt.

BABS: Oh good. Do you still shave your legs?

ALICE: How did you know I . . . Clean my legs?

BABS: Saw you in the bog at the House once. With a lady's razor. Not got that razor on you, have you?

ALICE: I'm afraid not.

BABS: Pity. Are all your family ginger on the body?

ALICE: Yes, actually.

BABS: Cold.

    (ALICE moves close and cradles him. A pause. BABS dead still, a long time. Then suddenly he's lively.)

    Are you wearing a corset?

ALICE: I don't think you should bother yourself . . .

BABS: Funny.

    The last information you take in. The last . . . Image to flit . . .

(Taps his head.)

Final insight. You are a corseted, ginger-haired, English fascist.

ALICE: And what are you?

BABS: Oh . . .

(A gesture, completed.)

I'm . . .

(He's dead. A pause. And the lights down.)

Scene Five

Bare stage. MARY there.

MARY: Day Jed came out, couldn't bear to go an' meet him.

Though, in a way, full of love for him.

But then, I've always had funny ways, like when I was a kid . . . Oh, picking up birds with bust legs. Nursing sick mice. Soppy, daft, funny ways. Asking for it. You know, your heart to break. Mouse dying, bird breakin' his other leg.

(A little laugh.)

That kind of thing. Soppy, daft, oh mushy things that you can't stand. And make you go cold inside.

(Quickly.)

Not that Jed's a bird with a bust . . . Jed's Jed. Just Jed. On his own way.

(Shrugs.)

Jed.

(A pause.)

But I told myself, I couldn't go. When they let him out. All night I was awake, tossing and turning, thinking of it, and I'd got the morning off work, and agreed with Cliff and V, when we would meet. Early, get the tube at eight. 'Cos they let them go, out through the little door in the gate.

(A little laugh.)

Million times I seen that, films, telly. Letting 'em go at nine, out the little door in the big door.

The bastards.

(A pause.)

I told myself I couldn't go, 'cos I was afraid. And I told myself I couldn't stand it, and would go cold inside.

(She goes off. A pause. CLIFF and V come on. He has a bottle of champagne.

(A pause. CLIFF glances at his watch. A pause. JED comes on. His head is shaved. CLIFF at once, cheerful.)

CLIFF: Christ Jed, what they done to your head?

(Nothing from JED. Silence. MARY comes on fast.)

MARY: Jed, told myself I couldn't come, then I couldn't . . . Not come. And I rushed!

They've cut your hair off.

(A pause.)

But you look nice.

(A pause.)

Jed.

(A pause. Uncertain.)

Jed?

(And the stage floods with red, awash with banners and songs.)

JED: Vlad?

(The effects growing.)

Vlad?

(LENIN appears at the back of the stage. He moves through his heroic gestures. A wind machine blows a gale across the stage. MARY, CLIFF, and V stand stock still through this passage.)

What do you make of it, Vladimir Ilyich?

LENIN: A noble, proletarian hatred for the bourgeois 'class politician' is the beginning of all wisdom.

JED: Right Vlad!

LENIN: Only a violent collision, which indeed may be forced upon the people, will wipe out the servility which has permeated the national consciousness.

JED: Yeh but, Vlad, yeh but . . .

(LENIN sweeping down the stage through many gestures.)

LENIN: Force! Force is the midwife of every old society which is pregnant with a new.

(JED, shouting over the gale.)

JED: Yeh but Vlad! Not got much here for you, Vlad! Little bit of hate. Dangerous intent. In my pocket somewhere, here, screwed up bit o' paper. Morsel of contempt. What I do with it Vlad? Help you out, little bit, little bit o' spite?

(LENIN sweeps past behind him.)

LENIN: Granite! Work!

(Diagonally back upstage.)

Work upon a granite theoretical foundation, legal and illegal, peaceful and stormy, open and underground, small circles and mass movements, parliamentary and terrorist.

(Right at the back now. The effects deepening.)

Left-wing communism is an infantile disorder. Politics is an art and a science that does not drop from the skies.

(He goes. The banners and songs, the gale cease. Still red light.)

JED: Yeh but, Vlad.

(Spreads his arms, mockingly.)

What can a poor boy do?

(Drops his arms and at once lights back to what they were before LENIN appeared. Pause. JED, angrily.)

Where's Will?

CLIFF: Couldn't get off work.

JED: You're lying through your teeth.

CLIFF: Will's . . .

JED: What?

(CLIFF shrugs.)

CLIFF: As ever.

JED: Tell him I want to see him. Tonight. Round our place.

(A pause.)

MARY: We got some champagne. 'Ere Cliff, what about the champagne?

(A pause.)

Celebration?

(Blackout.)

Scene Six

Lights up at once. Bare stage. WILL there. JED walks on.

WILL: Hello, old son.

(A pause.)

Jug bring on many changes?

JED: Some.

WILL: Little bird whispered to me, you been abusing your mind and your body. Speedy Gonzales?

(He giggles. No response from WILL.)

What were you trying to do? Elevate the whole of Brixton Gaol? Turn it upside down? Shake all the nasty creepy crawlies out? Every night I looked out my bedroom window, expecting to see . . . Whoosh! Brixton Gaol go by, spaceship to the stars, my old mate Jed for Captain.

(Suddenly embracing JED.)

Me old China. God, Jed, missed ya. 'Cor you're lovely, Jed. Sandpapered your nut down a bit, han't they? Still it's my old Jed's nut.

JED: For fucksake.

(JED shrugs him away.)

WILL: Sorry.

JED: What's the matter with you?

WILL: Dunno. I felt moved.

JED: You felt what?

WILL: At seeing you again.

JED: Well fuck you.

WILL: Jesus, Jed, I was only tickled to see you. Tickled pink, to see you.

JED: You gone soft in the head?

(A pause.)

WILL: Christ, oh Jesus. Jed? I'm getting all kinds of bad things from you. Jed?

(A pause.)

Oh Jesus.

(A pause.)

You were . . . I blush to say it, but you know, me and you, like . . .

(Fingers entwined.)

I mean you were beautiful.

(JED scoffs.)

Finicky. Bit tetchy. Bit of paranoia in there. But that was your way o' getting it together.

(Laughs.)

Jesus, I remember you spending all day, when we were setting up the occupation . . . All one Sunday, pouring out cups of water to reckon what we'd need. An' how you went on like an old woman, remember? 'Bout sleeping bags. And us all getting warm. Happy days, eh? Christ we were mad then, eh? Insane. It was great then, I mean we really . . . Didn't we?

(A pause.)

Eh?

(A pause.)

Wow.

(A pause.)

Jed?

(JED stares.)

Picking up a lot of static here, Jed . . .

JED: What's all this freaky talk, Will?

WILL: Freaky?

JED: Been to America, while I've been 'rotting in my cell'?

WILL: Hounslow actually. Moved in with a little chick, ta-tum ta ta. Substances
and dream machines under the floorboards, in the food. Can't have a slice
of bread an' marmite, without losing your mind. She's taken to injecting acid
in the eggs for breakfast now. We lead a very peaceful, domestic life.

JED: Do you know you're full of crap?

(WILL shrugs, tries to jolly things a little more . . .)

WILL: Yeh. Well . . .

(Fails. A pause.)

Jed, old son, changes, old son. Many changes . . . brought on. Y'know?

JED: Look at you.

(WILL looks about, perked up.)

WILL: Why, where am I?

JED: There, on the floor.

WILL: Oh yeh. Hello, Will.

JED: Hello, Will.

WILL: I think he's smashed out of his mind.

(Looks over 'himself' lying on the floor.)

Yeh, he's in a bad way. But he's smiling to 'imself. Maybe he's seeing things.
Think he's seeing things?

(He sniffs.)

He's not washed much. There's a distinctly underpantish whiff about this
dreamer.

(To JED.)

Yeh, he's far gone. Far away. Lotus eater.

But don't you think unkindly of him. Don't abuse 'im. If you come upon
'im, lying on the pavement, Piccadillypiccadilly, don't you kick 'im. Please
eh, Master? Pass 'im by, tiptoe.

'Cos his dreams are very fragile, Jed. Delicate. Precious. And his brain wall's thin, and liable to rupture, as a result of all the changes . . .

Jed?

JED: I remember a sharp little man.

WILL: Please don't, Jed.

JED: Childish. A talker. Got on your nerves.

WILL: Please don't, Jed.

JED: But loyal. Hard. Diamond at the core. Fearless.

WILL: Please don't, Jed.

JED: A sharp little man, who for all of his being a fool, did . . . I really do believe he did . . . Love the people. And had the guts to do a little about his love. And I'm standing here, looking down at what's left of him.

You got a daisy sewed on your arse?

WILL: Little bit o' colour.

JED: Bend over.

WILL: What?

JED: Bend over your fucking groovy arse, you fucking stinking little child of God.

WILL: Eh . . . Don't let's get heavy, Jed.

(JED grabs him by the neck.)

It's only a daisy. What you got against daisies? Unfair to daisies!

(JED rips the daisy off.)

JED: And the shirt.

WILL: What?

JED: Get that shirt off.

WILL: Not me Che shirt.

JED: And that.

(He tears a badge off WILL's jacket. Several tugs.)

WILL: No! No! No!

Not me Ho Chi Minh Memorial Badge!

JED: Shirt.

WILL: Worse than down at West End Central . . .

JED: Get that trash off.

(WILL jerks away from him.)

WILL: Whatsa matter with you?

JED: That obscene tat. Get it off. Get it off.

WILL: Alright alright!

JED: Get/it/all/off.

WILL: Alright!

> (He takes off his jacket, then his Che shirt. He crouches shivering, arms across himself. JED picks up the Che shirt, and crouches too. He stares morosely at the shirt.)

Speedy freak.

(A pause.)

That you?

(A pause.)

Eh?

(A pause.)

Rot your brain, that, Jed. Sored up yet, eh?

Speed freaks sore up fast.

'Course, Revolutionary drug, in't it. As recommended by the Weathermen. You are putting yourself in the big league. Speedy heavies. Like the Panthers, come down on their Harleys, to the beach . . . Dead of night . . . To meet Jean Genet, smuggle him into Amerika. And away they go into the dark . . . Eh?

I suppose I get the appeal.

Oh to be black, in black leather, on a black motor-bike, in the blackest night, Jean Genet on my pillion and my brain rotting away . . .

(A pause.)

Can I put my jacket on?

> (JED with a sharp movement turns the image of Guevara to WILL.)

JED: What's Mr Guevara to you?

WILL: Tee shirt.

> (Shrugs.)

I mean, it's just a tee shirt.

JED: There's a face on it.

WILL: Oh come on.

JED: Years ago, you'd have pissed on the very idea o' going about in this.

WILL: S' just a shirt.

JED: *What happened* to you?

WILL: S'just a shirt! Could be Marilyn Monroe on there, or Benny Hill.

(A pause.)

Mickey Mouse. Steve McQueen. Apollo moon landing. Stars an' stripes. Hammer an' Sickle.

(A pause.)

'S just a shirt.

JED: Got the poster of him dead?

WILL: What?

JED: This great man. This stupid, great man. Got the poster of him dead?

WILL: No, don't think so.

(Short pause.)

Hanging in our loo.

Sorry.

(He shrugs. JED throws the shirt, screwed up, at WILL. Who unravels it as he speaks.)

But you're coming on strong, Jed. Oh are you. Like some Sunday School teacher. Rapping me over the knuckles. Caught me pencilling a moustache on a picture o' Jesus. Rap rap. Naughty. O.K. O. K. you got busted.

O.K. that give you a halo? Come an' bash your old mates with? God given right?

I know you suffered. And all. Really though, I do.

Know.

Just maybe it's easier, sittin' in a cell. Having visions, Armageddons two a penny. Chalk 'em up on your ball an' chain, eh? Lurid scenarios.

But it's very hard, for us down in Hounslow . . . No not hard, that's insulting to you. Dreary. Dreary, day in day out. The jungles of Bolivia seem rather far away. Keeping a correct political point of view is something of a chore. Your mind begins to wander. I mean . . . I know when the milkman calls, you should grab him by the throat, and politicize him on the spot. But it's difficult. Specially if you owe him six weeks. An' you want your cornflakes soggy.

(He puts the shirt and the jacket back on. A pause. He's slumped, round shouldered.)

What happened to me?

(A pause.)

Nothing to it. Everyday life. All fervour gone.

One day, find yourself ranting on with the old, steamy enthusiasm 'bout something . . . Spectre of International Capitalism . . . And suddenly, urrgh. Sluch.

And you get smashed a bit, then most of the time. Millions are one way or the other. Smashed.

Urrgh. Sluch.

(A pause.)

JED: Come here.

(WILL stands and goes over to JED.)

Down here.

(WILL crouches down. JED slaps him in the face. Fairly hard, and repeatedly, but carefully — like someone bringing someone round, who's unconscious.)

You and I.

(Slap.)

Are going on a little journey.

(Slap.)

WILL: Oh yeh.

(He flinches. A slap.)

JED: Wake up.

(Slap.)

WILL: I am awake.

(Slap.)

JED: Wake up.

(Slap.)

WILL: Stop it.

(Slap.)

What you doing?

JED: You and I.

(Slap.)

Are going to the West Country.

WILL: That's nice.

(Slap.)

Where? Bristol, Bath?

(Slap.)

JED: Never mind where.

(Slap.)

You got bread?

(Slap.)

WILL: Yeh.

(Slap.)

For the fare?

JED: Right.

WILL: Yeh.

(Slap.)

JED: And fifty quid.

(Slap.)

WILL: What you want fifty quid for?

(Slap.)

Stop hitting me in my face.

JED: Can you get the fifty quid?

(Slap.)

WILL: Don't hit me in my face.

(JED grabs him by the shoulders.)

JED: Can you get fifty pounds.

WILL: Yeh. Maybe I'll deal or something . . .

JED: By the weekend.

WILL: Dicy. I'll try. But what for?

(Slap.)

Don't do that!

(He hits JED back. JED grabs WILL's hand by the wrist, tight.)

JED: Why, old son. Can't you guess?

WILL: Surprise me.

JED: You and I are going to change the world.

WILL: Really? That will be a nice . . . Surprise.

(A pause.)

Can I have my wrist back, please?

(And at once lights down fast. JED still holding his wrist.)

Scene Seven

Lights up at once. At the front. Bare stage. MARY, VERONICA and CLIFF.

MARY: Don't wanna talk about it.

VERONICA: You're being a silly little cow.

MARY: Don't wanna. Won't.

VERONICA: Mary . . .

MARY: Want some tea?

VERONICA: No.

MARY: Want some tea, Cliff?

(CLIFF shakes his head. A pause.)

VERONICA: Anyway, when will they be back?

MARY: Said they'd be back yesterday.

VERONICA: Have you heard from them?

MARY: Why should I?

(A door slams. JED and WILL come out of the dark. Pause.)

We been arguing about you. They think . . . Well they think.

JED: Do they.

VERONICA: Go far?

(JED stares at her. Then turns to WILL. Who takes off his haversack carefully, helped by JED. They take a biscuit tin out of the lid. Haversack. JED takes off the lid, carefully. Then sits back on his haunches looking at VERONICA. WILL gives a short giggle.)

Wow. Shazzaam. Kerpow.

(A pause.)

That what you want me to say?

(A pause.)

MARY: What is it? What they got there?

(VERONICA, straight at JED.)

VERONICA: Gelignite, sticks of gelignite that's all, nothing but sticks of gelignite. Silly fireworks. Make a big bang, that's all. One big bang, and after all that, silence. Nothing really to concern yourself with. Just big bangers.

MARY: Gelignite?

(A pause.)

WILL: Don't think that lady's gonna come on our picnic, Jed. 'Fraid o' creepy crawlies in the cucumber sandwiches.

(He giggles uneasily. A pause. JED looks at CLIFF.)

CLIFF: No.

(A pause.)

Oh no. Not that. There's only one way, time was you knew it, Jed. Work, corny work, with and for the people. Politicizing them and learning from them, everyone of them. Millions. O.K. O.K. come a time you'll have to go out there.

(Sharp gesture, his fingers as a gun.)

But only with the people, as a people's army, borne along by them. You know all this, Jed, we've worked together . . . You know you are, right now, there . . . A nothing. Zero. A crank with a tin box of bangs. I dunno, I dunno

. . . That you've degenerated, oh come down to this, Jed. Some fucking stupid gesture . . .

(He scoffs.)

An explosion! And they'll call you a 'Revolutionary' of some kind, but a 'Revolutionary.' You know what a mockery that will be.

(A pause as JED carefully packs the gelignite and tin away in the haversack, and helps it onto WILL's back. They're going, upstage into the dark. But at the last moment JED turns, and speaks to CLIFF.)

JED: Went to see a terrible film once. Carpet-baggers. With Carole Baker. Right load of old tat, going on up there on the big silver screen. Boring, glossy tat, untouchable being on the silver screen.

And there was this drunk in the front row. With a bottle of ruby wine. And did he take exception to the film, he roared and screamed. Miss Baker above all, came in for abuse. Something about her got right up his nose.

So far up, that he was moved to chuck his bottle of ruby wine right through Miss Baker's left tit.

The left tit moved on in an instant, of course. But for the rest of the film, there was that bottle shaped hole.

(With a jab of his finger.)

Clung. One blemish on the screen. But somehow you couldn't watch the film from then.

And so thinks . . .

(With a bow.)

The poor bomber. Bomb 'em. Again and again. Right through their silver screen. Disrupt the spectacle. The obscene parade, bring it to a halt! Scatter the dolly girls, let advertisements bleed . . . Bomb 'em, again and again! Murderous display. An entertainment for the oppressed, so they may dance a little, take a little warmth from the sight, eh?

(He laughs.)

Go down into the mire eh? Embrace the butcher, eh?

(A silence.)

Think on't.

(He goes.)

MARY: Jed?

(A pause.)

Yeh, I'll make some tea. Anyone want me make some tea?

CLIFF: Yes.

(VERONICA puts her arm round MARY. The lights go down fast.)

Scene Eight

Bare stage. WILL at the back, the lights narrowed upon him. He speaks aside.

WILL: All night. Walked about London. Hours and hours of talk. And so
tired. And Jed going on and on. Re-lentless. Burning it all up.

And mid-morning, train from Euston Station. Lovely day. Into Hertfordshire.
Got off at a little station. And 'ouses, and gardens . . . In the Indian Summer
lovely weather. And we walked for miles, over the fields, in the lanes. Jed
like he was on a laser beam. Through the English Countryside. Burning on
and on.

To here.

(At once lights up all over the stage. JED comes on.)

JED: The man's garden!

WILL: I'm so hot. Abathe in me own exhaust fumes. Fuckin' 'ell! Aren't the
trees high.

JED: All we've got to do is relax. Sun ourselves. And he'll be out, doing his
garden.

WILL: Yeh.

(A pause.)

Jed, Jed . . . With that . . . Load, do you think the grass'll burn? And there'll
be a gale won't there. Shake all the petals off the rhododendrons. The birds'll
rise for miles around.

(A pause.)

I wonder if the air, y'know the oxygen in the air, that'll burn too . . . God
Jed I wish I was smashed out of my mind. I could do with it, I could do with
it right now . . . In the English Countryside. In the Indian Summer weather.
Yer English lanes. Burning, burning, burning on and on . . .

(Suddenly.)

Jed I'm sick scared!

JED: Sun . . . Ourselves.

WILL: Yeh. Right.

(A pause.)

Funny.

JED: What?

WILL: My old Dad was a gardener. Dead sure this isn't the time of year
rhododendrons are meant to . . . Y'know, flower.

(A pause.)

Oh I'm so tired.

(Change.)

'Ere! Maybe 'e forces the rhododendrons out by torture. Yeh.

(A pause.)

Look at the . . . Lawn. Look at the . . . Trees. Look at the . . . Flowers. Look at the . . . Chimneys o' the 'ouse . . . Look at the . . . Fucking English Garden 'e's got.

(Off stage a motor starts. ALICE glides the length of the stage on a lawn-mower with an attached seat. A watering can hangs on the handlebars. He's slumped rather badly. He's off. The motor stops. A pause.)

Far out.

(A pause.)

Utterly amazing.

(A pause.)

Eh, Jed.

JED: Shut up. And watch him.

WILL: Cat and mouse? Meow we are the black cat gang with red claws.

JED: Just SHUT UP.

(The lawn-mower's motor heard off stage again. ALICE drives the lawn-mower on and down stage. JED and WILL crouch down at the side of the stage. ALICE stops the lawn-mower. A pause. He speaks aside.)

ALICE: The old fool, died in my arms. I think he'd sent for me, that day, not necessarily to do that . . . Though he was prone to what he called scenarios. Rigged niceties of behaviour. Genteel excesses.

Punted his dead body back along the river in the dusk. Lost half the deposit for being out late. The boatman haggled, 'til he realized. Taking Babs out of the punt one leg of his corpse . . Got wet. There was a smell. His viciousness and cunning knew no end.

And going over the events of that day . . . I think he set out to destroy my peace of mind. And going over the events of that day, I feel . . . Perhaps he succeeded only too well. Set off a chain of thoughts. Self-realizations?

And now?

(A helpless gesture.)

At a loss. With a kind of self loathing. That old man! His last day alive. He treated me like an old lover. I felt . . . Curiously dirtied.

I knew he bitterly opposed me in the party, and my friends. Set me up, but in the later days, did all he could against me. Bitterly . . . That last day could have been one long, last political act . . . The old High Tory's last throw at me. That viciousness and cunning.

(Something catches his eye on the ground before him.)

Oh bloody weeds.

(He gets off the mower with the watering can and waters the weeds. JED and WILL rise with kids' Indian yodels . . . Very fast this . . . And over-power ALICE. JED handcuffs him, hands behind his back.)

JED: Mask get the mask!

WILL: Right the mask!

JED: With the funny grin!

WILL: Right right!

(WILL goes over and gets the haversack.)

ALICE: What do you . . . What do you hope to achieve . . .

JED: Shut up!

ALICE: What possible end!

JED: *The* end, mate!

(To WILL.)

Right!

(WILL takes out a string of gelignite from the haversack, with a short ignitable fuse. It's arranged round a sack. JED and WILL hold it up carefully. ALICE flinches away.)

Peace!

ALICE: What?

JED: In peace! Understand?

ALICE: I'm sorry?

(JED lets ALICE see he has a knife. ALICE nods. They put the mask over ALICE's head. A pause. Then JED and WILL look at each other. WILL gives a little giggle. Stops. JED lights the fuse. ALICE gives little jerks of his head in panic, side to side, but mute. The moment JED lights the fuse WILL grabs the haversack and runs upstage. JED takes a few steps away upstage but suddenly stops, stares at ALICE, then crouches down again. WILL realizes JED is not following and skids to a stop.)

WILL: Jed.

JED: Get away.

WILL: Jed, it's burning!

JED: Get off.

WILL: Jed, thirty seconds there'll be a meat haze.

JED: I said . . . Get!

WILL: Molecules. Just a smell of the breeze . . .

(A pause.)

Oh.

(Backing away.)

Oh, Jed.

(Backing away.)

Oh no, oh, Jed.

(Backing away.)

You were, oh Jed.

(He stops. A pause. Then he turns and runs. Let the fuse burn right out. A long pause. Nothing happens.)

ALICE: Could you . . .

(A pause.)

Could you tell me what's happening out there?

(JED, quietly.)

JED: Oh Mr Public Man here we are.

ALICE: I'm sorry?

JED: It's alright. The fuse failed.

ALICE: What did you say?

JED: Fuse failed.

ALICE: What?

(JED shouts.)

JED: I said . . . The fuse failed.

ALICE: Ah.

(ALICE, little twitches of his head, which he brings under control.)

Is it going off or isn't it?

JED: I don't know.

ALICE: What did you say?

JED: I don't know.

ALICE: What?

(JED shouts.)

JED: I said . . . I don't know if it's going off or not.

ALICE: Ah.

(ALICE, little twitches of his head, which he brings under control.)

Perhaps you should try another fuse.

JED: Not got one.

ALICE: What?

(A long pause.)

Look I do think it's your move.

JED: Do you.

(JED shouts.)

Do you.

(A pause. Then JED goes and takes the gelignite mask off. ALICE's face twitches badly. He turns his head aside, closes his eyes, controls it.)

ALICE: And now? A knifing? 'The boot'?

(A pause.)

Perhaps a strangulation?

(JED shrugs.)

Please let me know. Sooner or later.

JED: I don't know.

ALICE: I am a rather nervous man. Perhaps you could make your mind up.

JED: I'm doing my best.

ALICE: I'm sure you are.

JED: Oh Christ.

ALICE: Indeed.

JED: What . . .

(A pause.)

What did you do to the rhododendrons?

ALICE: Do you mean why should they be in flower this time of year? Forced feeding. Chemicals. A second flowering.

JED: Why not?

ALICE: Will you . . .

JED: *I don't know!*

ALICE: I have fibrositis, you see. Under the right shoulder blade . . .

(He falters.)

Bubbles on the muscle.

JED: Alright alright!

(ALICE with open panic.)

ALICE: Don't, don't, don't harm me . . .

(He controls himself. A pause. He moves his shoulder. Then indicates the mask with his foot.)

What is this?

JED: Industrial gelignite.

ALICE: With a burning fuse?

JED: Any objections?

ALICE: No no . . . I just seem to remember from the war one is much better advised to use an electrical charge, from a battery. Where did you get this?

JED: Off a man.

ALICE: Quarry man?

(JED shrugs.)

Looks like he sold you a pig in a poke.

JED: Looks like that.

ALICE: You don't seem to mind.

JED: No?

ALICE: You're a very sullen young man.

JED: I 'have my troubles'.

ALICE: Don't we all. I mean I'm very glad you were fobbed off with . . . Dud goods. I seem to owe my life to a dishonest trader of the criminal classes. Though what comfort there is in that, I'm not quite sure. But you seem quite unconcerned at the . . . Failure of your escapade. Perhaps it's the thought that counts?

JED: Why not?

ALICE: The politics of gesture. I know all about that. The Special Branch ran a Summer School Course on Revolutionary Theory the other summer. Let me see what you are . . .

(He falters.)

'Into,' as they say. Situationist theory?

JED: Really?

ALICE: A violent intervention. A disruption. A spectacle against the spectacle. A firework in the face of the Ruling Class.

JED: Sounds fun.

ALICE: How did you come to choose me to be a . . . Roman candle in the Revolutionary Struggle.?

JED: Housing. Once upon a time I . . . Had a concern for housing. And you're in the Ministry of the Environment.

ALICE: I am not.

(A pause.)

JED: Oh come on.

ALICE: I am in the Office of the Paymaster General.

JED: Don't piss about.

ALICE: There was a Cabinet Reshuffle. I was moved downstairs. How incredibly inefficient of you not to know.

JED: Oh I wish I'd blown your head off, you bloody and you arrogant man.

ALICE: You do me an injustice. Apart from the obvious injustice of trying to blow my head off. I am not a bloody and an arrogant man.

JED: What do you see yourself as, then? Queer, failed and fifty?

ALICE: Perceptive little bitch.

(ALICE, suddenly angry.)

You young thug. I'm trying to be brave.

JED: So am I!

ALICE: Some dignity . . . You must allow.

JED: Me too.

ALICE: Yes, yes of course . . . Though I don't see why.

JED: I could beat you, I could beat you now!

ALICE: C . . . Come on then!

JED: Oh Christ!

ALICE: Kick me. Where are you? Come up behind me. Kick my spine. Go for the nervous system, boy. Total pain. Or be witty, go for the hair, get me by the hair . . . Get your fingers in my eyes, oh Dear God . . . Take me apart with your hands you hoodlum. You young, brutal, would-be change the worlder.

JED: Christ, Christ!

ALICE: You've got me in your hands. Isn't that what you want? What you hate, in your hands. To tear. A butchering job on the World. That it, that it, young man?

JED: Oh Christ!

(ALICE, suddenly quietly.)

ALICE: Jed? . . . Your friend who ran away, called you Jed? Jed, we seem to have reached a state of . . . Balance. Either you butcher me, or we stay out here all night. The evenings are drawing in. Chilly. Heavy . . .

(He falters.)

Dew.

JED: Sun'll still be hot for a bit.

(JED lies back, his hands under his head. A pause.)

ALICE: A friend of mine died.

(A pause.)

I know you . . . Hold me, in some way personally responsible. For what I don't know. The World's ills? Some particular event? Or just, perhaps, for being in public life? Having dirty hands? No . . . Purity of intent. Is that what you see yourself as having? Purity of intent? No doubt you do. How dreadfully unfair.

(A pause.)

For being myself? For being me? The terrorist's vendetta, there's no answer
to it, then. It may come from anywhere. Perhaps you've had a bad life.
Have you had a bad life? I would like to know. Because you may yet decide
to assault me, and it is very easy to injure . . . It would be a mild comfort
Jed, if the balance is going to tip . . . And you are going to come at me and
kick me . . .

(He swallows.)

Why?

JED: Oh, Mr Public Man.

(JED stands up. ALICE flinches. But JED releases ALICE from the handcuffs.)

ALICE: Thank you. You couldn't . . . Give my shoulder blade a rub could you?

(JED ignores that and picks up the gelignite mask.)

JED: Dunno. I dunno. Can't get rid. Can't shake it off. Magnificence, that it
would be magnificent to have you bleeding on the lawn.

ALICE: I can't understand that. Dear God. How can any human being understand that?

JED: No. I do. Late, late summer, musky smell from the FUCKING RHODO-
DENDRONS. An English garden with it's Englishman. Done at last. DONE.
Oh Mr I am deeply in contempt of you. All of you. Bubbles is it, in the
muscle? Your nails, hair, little bits. And your mind. I am deeply in contempt
of your English mind. There is BLAME THERE. That wrinkled stuff with
the picture of English Life in its pink, rotten meat. In your head. And the
nasty tubes to your eyes that drip Englishness over everything you see. The
cool, glycerine humanity of your tears that smarms our ANGER. I am deeply
in contempt of your FUCKING HUMANITY. The goo, the sticky mess of
your English humanity that gums up our ears to your lies, our eyes to your
crimes . . . I dunno, I dunno, what can a . . . What can a . . . Do? To get it
real. And get it real to you. And get at you, Mr English Public Man, with
oh yeh the spectacle, the splendour of you magnificently ablaze for the
delight and encouragement of all your enemies . . . I dunno I dunno . . . So
I thought . . .

(He raises the mask.)

A little danger. Into our sad.

(JED lowers the mask. Hangs his head. A pause. ALICE stands.)

ALICE: Drink?

(Nothing from JED.)

Would you like a drink?

JED: What?

ALICE: I'll go into the house, and bring a drink out. Be a lovely . . . Early evening. On the lawn.

JED: You'll phone the police.

ALICE: Perhaps. But then . . . We could both do with a drink. Scotch? Long, with ice? I'll bring a tray out.

(Uneasily.)

End up sloshed together.

(A pause.)

Once I was eager to . . . How shall I say, 'Claw at the World?'

(JED, softly.)

JED: Christ.

ALICE: There is no reason why we should not attempt some kind of . . . Humane resolution . . . Between us.

JED: There is every reason.

ALICE: I'm sorry, didn't quite catch . . .

(JED shakes his head.)

Drink anyway.

(JED raises the mask.)

JED: The gelly. Oh why, why couldn't, just once . . . Couldn't it be real?

(JED throws the mask to the floor.
At once an explosion and blackout.
Three seconds silence.
Lights up.
Upstage the JED and ALICE actors lie faces down. There's something strange about the position of JED's arm. Smoke dirfts over them. CLIFF is standing downstage at the edge of the stage. He speaks aside.)

CLIFF: Jed. The waste. I can't forgive you that.

(A pause.)

The waste of your anger. Not the murder, murder is common enough. Not the violence, violence is everyday. What I can't forgive you Jed, my dear, dead friend, is the waste.

(Blackout.)